MINEHEAD
TAU
04/25

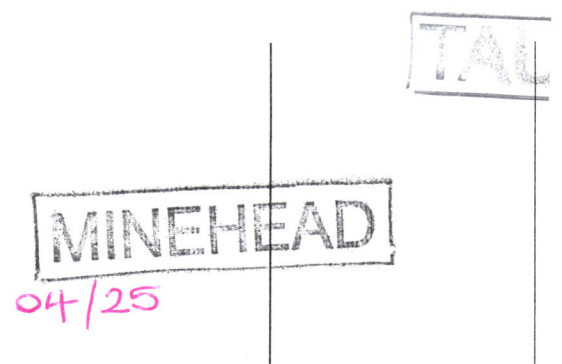

GW01337029

Please return/renew this item by the last date shown on this label, or on your self-service receipt.

To renew this item, visit **www.librarieswest.org.uk**, use the LibrariesWest app, or contact your library.

Your Borrower Number and PIN are required.

LibrariesWest

2 1 0044255 4

FACING YOUR FEARS

FACING YOUR FEAR OF GOING TO A NEW SCHOOL

BY RENEE BIERMANN

raintree
a Capstone company — publishers for children

Raintree is an imprint of Capstone Global Library Limited, a company incorporated in England and Wales having its registered office at 264 Banbury Road, Oxford, OX2 7DY – Registered company number: 6695582

www.raintree.co.uk
myorders@raintree.co.uk

Hardback edition text © Capstone Global Library Limited 2024
Paperback edition text © Capstone Global Library Limited 2025

The moral rights of the proprietor have been asserted. All rights reserved. No part of this publication may be reproduced in any form or by any means (including photocopying or storing it in any medium by electronic means and whether or not transiently or incidentally to some other use of this publication) without the written permission of the copyright owner, except in accordance with the provisions of the Copyright, Designs and Patents Act 1988 or under the terms of a licence issued by the Copyright Licensing Agency, 5th Floor, Shackleton House, 4 Battle Bridge Lane, London, SE1 2HX (www.cla.co.uk). Applications for the copyright owner's written permission should be addressed to the publisher.

Editorial credits
Editor: Erika L. Shores; Designer: Dina Her; Media Researcher: Jo Miller; Production Specialist: Tori Abraham

ISBN 978 1 3982 4999 8 (hardback)
ISBN 978 1 3982 4998 1 (paperback)

British Library Cataloguing in Publication Data
A full catalogue record for this book is available from the British Library.

Acknowledgements
Getty Images: Ariel Skelley, 17, Blend Images - LWA/Dann Tardif, 19, JGI/Jamie Grill, 5, shylendrahoode, 7, SolStock, 8, 11, vgajic, 9; Shutterstock: Domira (background), cover and throughout, mangpor2004, Cover, Kapitosh (cloud), cover and throughout, Marish (brave girl), cover and throughout, Monkey Business Images, 14, 18, Robert Kneschke, 13, Tetiana Maslovska, 21, TinnaPong, 6, wavebreakmedia, 12, 15

Every effort has been made to contact copyright holders of material reproduced in this book. Any omissions will be rectified in subsequent printings if notice is given to the publisher.

All the internet addresses (URLs) given in this book were valid at the time of going to press. However, due to the dynamic nature of the internet, some addresses may have changed, or sites may have changed or ceased to exist since publication. While the author and publisher regret any inconvenience this may cause readers, no responsibility for any such changes can be accepted by either the author or the publisher.

Printed and bound in India.

CONTENTS

New school fears 4

Gathering information............................. 8

Finding your way 10

Making new friends 12

Asking for help with schoolwork........ 16

    Picture yourself calm 20

    Glossary 22

    Find out more 23

    Index... 24

    About the author........................... 24

Words in **bold** are in the glossary.

NEW SCHOOL FEARS

Going to a new school is a big change. You might worry about getting lost. You might be **nervous** about making friends.

It's okay to have these fears. But you can work through them. You can face your fears about your new school. Soon, you will be learning and having fun.

5

New things can cause **anxiety**. Anxiety is a feeling. Think of it as a big storm. Maybe it rains hard. Maybe there are high winds. But then the storm passes. No storm lasts forever. The wind and rain stop. The sun comes out again.

This is how anxiety works too. Anxious feelings don't last forever. You will stop worrying. You will feel good again.

7

GATHERING INFORMATION

What can you do before you go to your new school? You can ask questions. Find out your school's name. Ask if you can visit the school in person or see it online. Ask how many classmates you will have.

Knowing information will help you feel more **secure**. It can also help you get excited. Look at a map of your school. Learn your teacher's name.

FINDING YOUR WAY

You might be afraid you will get lost. This fear is normal. Schools have many rooms. But schools also have people! Teachers and **support staff** are there to help you find your way around.

Look for an adult. Ask, "Can you help me?" Explain what you need. It is **brave** to ask for help when you need it. It shows **courage**.

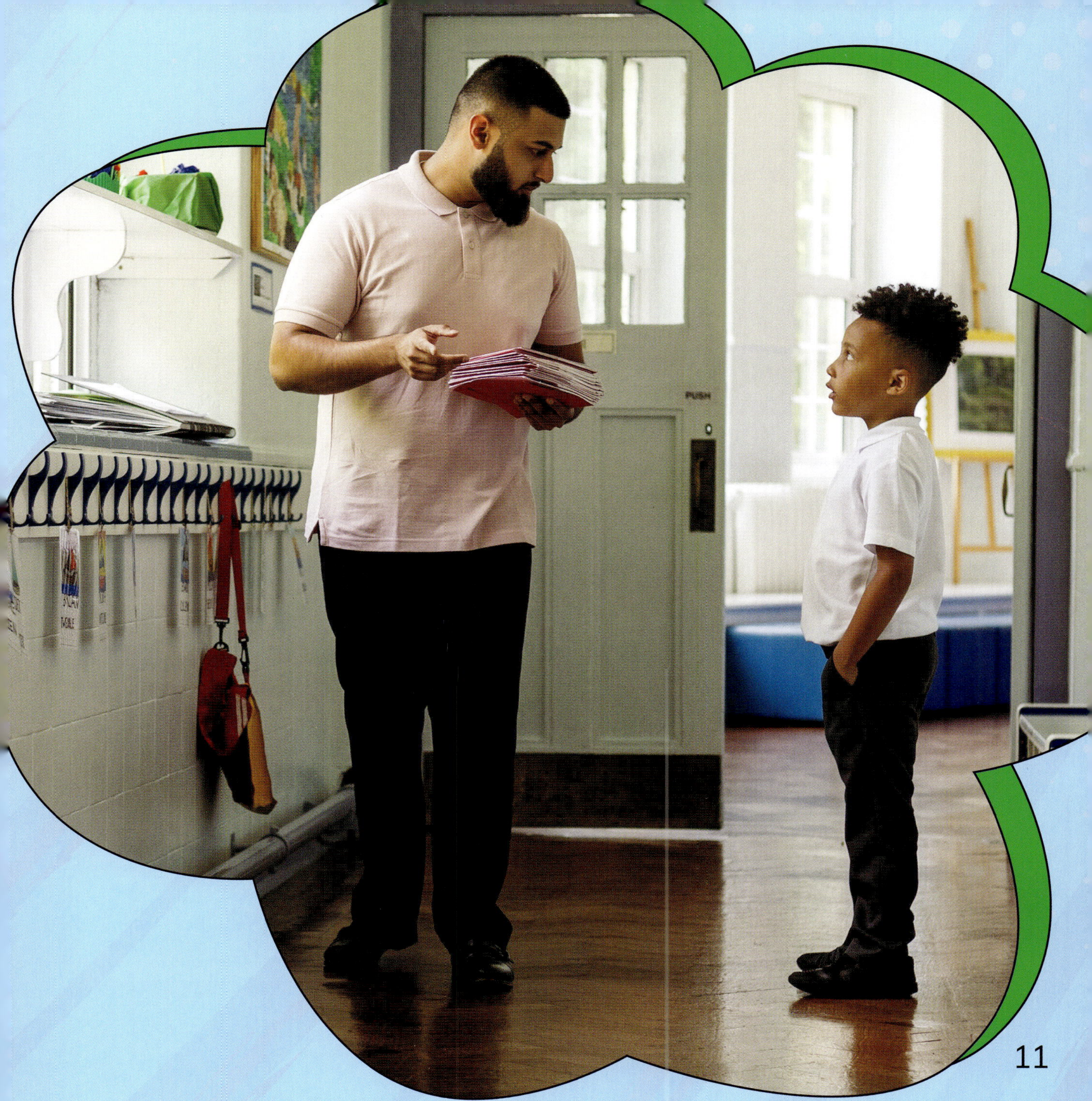
PUSH

MAKING NEW FRIENDS

Your new school has children just like you. They are your classmates. You are all learning together. You might work in groups. You might work with partners. Each day, you will feel more **comfortable**.

Show your classmates that you care. They might have fears about school too. You can make them feel better. You can be the fun, new friend for someone else!

13

How can you make more friends? Ask others to sit with you at lunch. Invite classmates to play with you at break time.

Sharing information helps friendships grow. Tell new friends about your favourite things. If you are worried, tell your friends how you feel. Ask your friends to share their favourite things and feelings too. This will make your friendships stronger.

ASKING FOR HELP WITH SCHOOLWORK

Are you worried about schoolwork? Remind yourself you do not have to learn alone. Your teachers will help you. They're excited to teach you. You'll also have tools to help you learn. Some tools are books and videos.

Remember that learning takes time. It will become easier. And school is not all just work. There is time to play and have fun too.

17

What can you do if you **struggle** with schoolwork? Be brave. Ask for help. Here are some ways to ask for help:

How do I _____?

Can you explain _____?

Can you help me understand _____?

Finally, remember that a new school isn't new forever. You will get to know your teachers. You will find new friends. And your fears will be in the past!

PICTURE YOURSELF CALM

Are you still nervous? Drawing a picture will help you feel calm and brave.

What you need
- paper
- crayons or felt-tip pens

What you do

1. Draw a line down the middle of a piece of paper.

2. On the left side, draw yourself now. Show yourself feeling anxious about your new school. Add details, such as dark clouds and rain, to help describe how you're feeling.

3. On the right side, draw yourself in the future. Show yourself feeling happy at your new school. Add some details like a friendly teacher, a smiling classmate and the sun shining on the playground.

4. Hang your picture where you will see it often. Imagine yourself on the happy side. Imagine being comfortable and having fun at your new school.

Look at your picture when you feel anxious. Remind yourself that anxiety passes.

GLOSSARY

anxiety feeling of worry or fear

brave strong and powerful

comfortable feeling relaxed and not worried

courage strength to get through something that is hard

nervous feeling anxious and worried

secure safe and happy

struggle have a hard time with something

support staff people who work at a school, such as teaching assistants, lunchtime workers and office workers

Find Out More

Books

Being a Good Friend (Mind Matters), Mari Schuh (Raintree, 2022)

Making Friends: A Book About First Friendships, Amanda McCardie (Walker Books, 2021)

Sometimes I Feel Worried (Name Your Emotions), Jaclyn Jaycox (Raintree, 2022)

Websites

www.bbc.co.uk/cbeebies/watch/whats-the-big-idea-friends
This CBeebies video shows how friends can be different from each other.

www.youtube.com/watch?v=ReMq3KX8F94
Watch this video to find out what makes a good friend.

INDEX

anxiety 6

asking questions 8, 10, 18

classmates 8, 12, 14

getting lost 4, 10

making friends 4, 12, 14, 15, 19

nervousness 4

schoolwork 16, 18

support staff 10

teachers 9, 10, 16, 19

worrying 4, 6, 15

ABOUT THE AUTHOR

Renee Biermann enjoys writing books for children. She started many new schools throughout her life. At each one, she found amazing teachers and good friends. She also learned so many new things!